paint

Starting Out...

 The activities are designed for adults and children to do together. With a closet or a box full of craft supplies and a spare ten minutes, it's amazing what you can create!

 The activities should take about ten minutes once the materials have been assembled. Every child is different and often a project is worth continuing beyond the time limit.

 Step-by-step instructions are usually followed by examples showing how to extend the activities. If you don't have the exact materials, use anything suitable you have on hand.

 Warning: All steps involving scissors or sharp objects should be performed by adults, not children.

Paint Practice

Why not start young children off with some simple color mixing. Even before they can hold a brush, they can have fun mixing paints with their fingers and discovering what colors they produce. Try out some of these color combinations:

Red and yellow

Red and blue

Red and white

Red and green

Blue and yellow

Black and white

Paint Closet

Keep a closet full of supplies for your paint activities.

Essentials
If you only have a few painting materials at home, these are the ones to collect: brightly colored poster paints, paint brushes, scissors, paper, poster board, glue, and tape.

Luxury Items
Glitter, sequins, clear glaze, pipe cleaners, tissue paper, and pompoms are some of the many supplies that will add magic to your child's artwork!

Things to Collect
Recycle everyday items such as cardboard tubes, egg cartons, string, and yarn for all your paint activities.

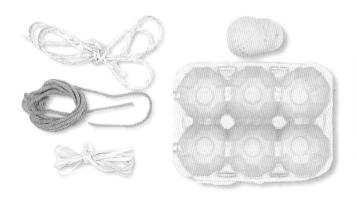
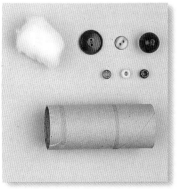

Step-by-step Drawings

Help your child learn to draw by breaking a picture down into its basic shapes.

Pig

1 Make a circle.

2 Draw two circles for eyes and an oval nose.

3 Add two upside-down triangles for the ears.

Dinosaur

1 Draw a semi-circle.

2 Add some triangles to the curved top line.

3 Put two squares for the legs and a dot for the eye.

Truck

1 Draw a rectangle.

2 Put one rectangle inside another one for the cab.

3 Add two circles for the truck's wheels.

Simple Pictures

See if your child can figure out what shapes are in these pictures too.

Cat

Dog

Fish

Flower

Ladybug

Tree

Boat

Rocket

Car

Body Printing

You will need: paint, paint brush, paper, hands, and feet!

Hand Prints
Brush some paint onto the hand. Press it firmly on a sheet of paper.

Rainbow Prints
Paint bands of color directly onto the hand and press it firmly onto a piece of paper.

Footprints
Why not try printing with your feet too!

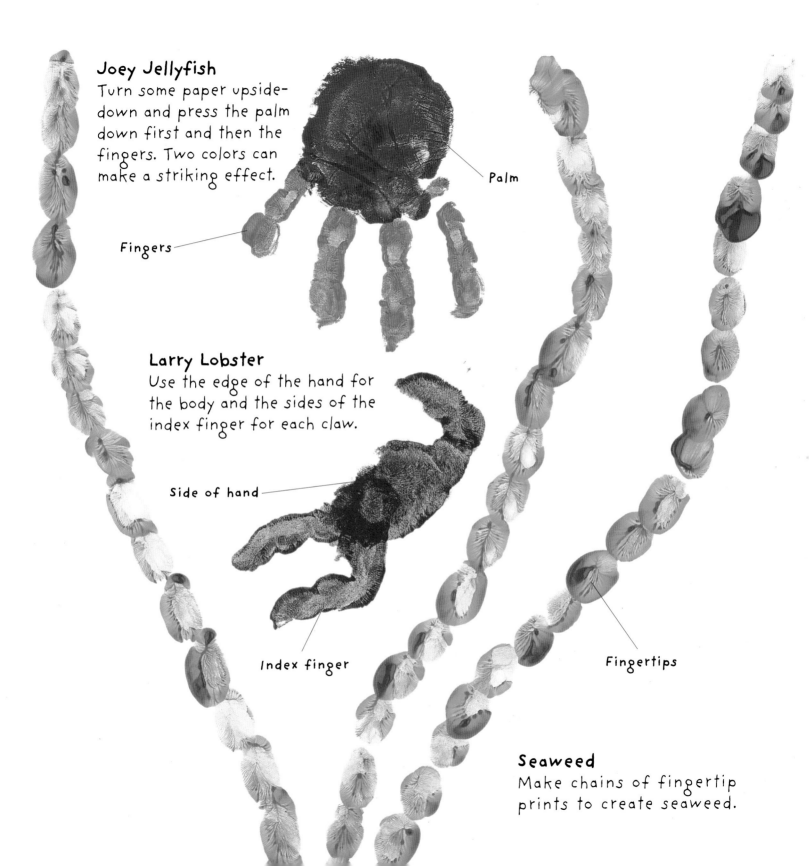

Joey Jellyfish

Turn some paper upside-down and press the palm down first and then the fingers. Two colors can make a striking effect.

Palm

Fingers

Larry Lobster

Use the edge of the hand for the body and the sides of the index finger for each claw.

Side of hand

Index finger

Fingertips

Seaweed

Make chains of fingertip prints to create seaweed.

Finger Painting

You will need: paper, brightly colored paints, and fingers!

Caterpillar

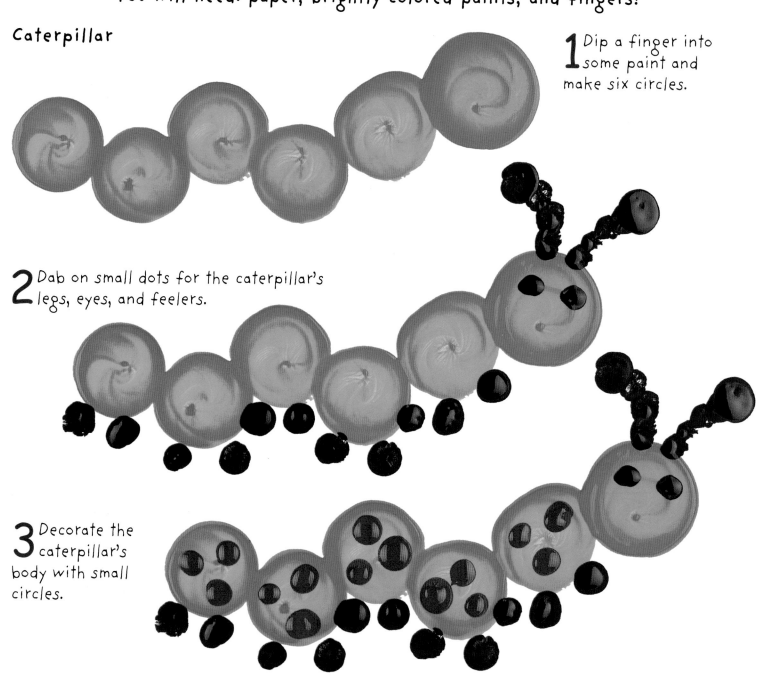

1 Dip a finger into some paint and make six circles.

2 Dab on small dots for the caterpillar's legs, eyes, and feelers.

3 Decorate the caterpillar's body with small circles.

Spider

1 Paint a large blue circle for the spider's body.

2 Paint eight curved lines for the legs.

3 Add dots for the eyes and eight more for the "feet"!

Snail

1 Paint a green circle over a yellow one for the shell.

2 Draw a curved line for the head and body.

3 Dab on an eye and small black dots for the feelers.

Butterfly

1 For wings, paint four ovals joined at the center.

2 Add a body with two dots above it.

3 Dab some colored spots on the wings.

More Finger Painting

You will need: colored paints, fabric or poster board with holes, glitter, and fingers!

Frog

 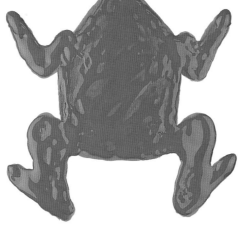 

1 Paint a square with a triangle on top of it.

2 Add two curved front and two curved back legs.

3 Give the frog some dots on its back and two eyes.

Turtle

 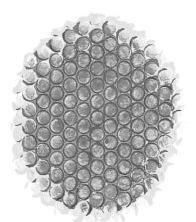 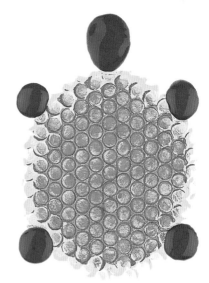

1 Put heavy paper or fabric with holes in it onto paper. Paint a yellow oval through it.

2 When it is dry, paint a green oval on top using the paper or fabric stencil.

3 Finally, dab on four circles for the legs and one bigger one for the head.

Dragonfly

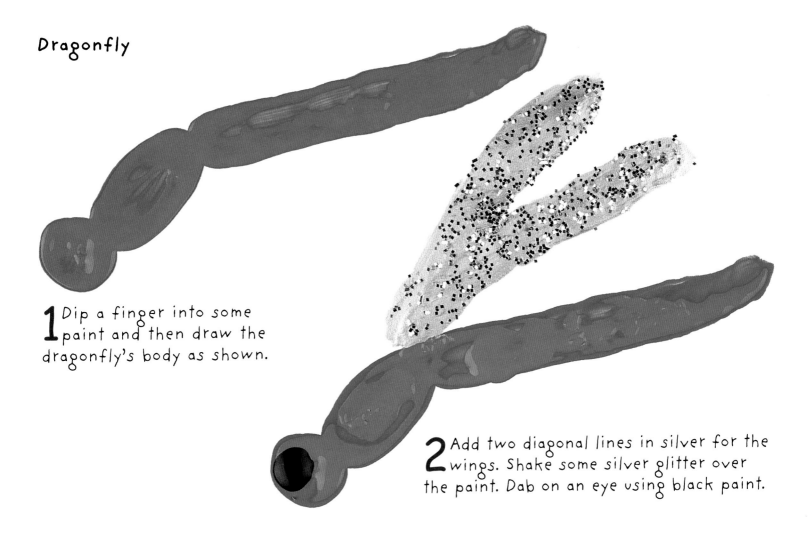

1 Dip a finger into some paint and then draw the dragonfly's body as shown.

2 Add two diagonal lines in silver for the wings. Shake some silver glitter over the paint. Dab on an eye using black paint.

Goldfish

1 Paint a yellow oval attached to a yellow triangle to create this fish shape.

2 Mix red paint with the yellow. Give the fish an eye and add some glitter.

Mirror Pictures

You will need: paints, paper, and a paint brush.

1 Fold a piece of paper in half. Open it out and paint half a butterfly centered on the folded line.

2 Fold the paper along the center line again. Press down firmly so the paint spreads onto the other side.

3 Open the paper to reveal the complete butterfly picture.

Mirror image made by folding the paper in half

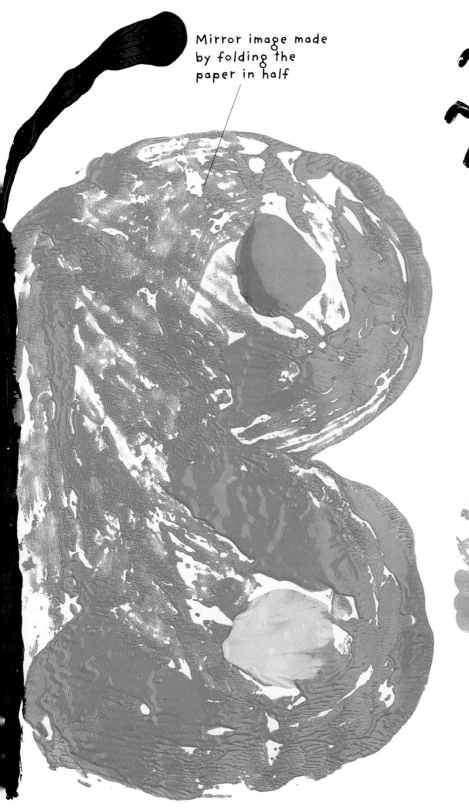

Letitia Ladybug
You could also try simple fish, spider, kite, bee, flower, or leaf mirror pictures as well.

Oliver Owl
Make an owl from two semicircles, a claw, and an eye. Glue sequins on both wings.

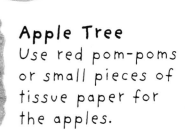

Apple Tree
Use red pom-poms or small pieces of tissue paper for the apples.

Painting Faces

You will need: paper plate, pencil, paints, paint brush, paper, scissors, and cotton balls.

1 Draw a clown's face onto the back of a paper plate.

2 Leave the features white and paint the rest pink.

3 Now paint the clown's nose and mouth.

4 Add paper circles for eyes and paint on some freckles. Cotton ball eyebrows complete this funny face!

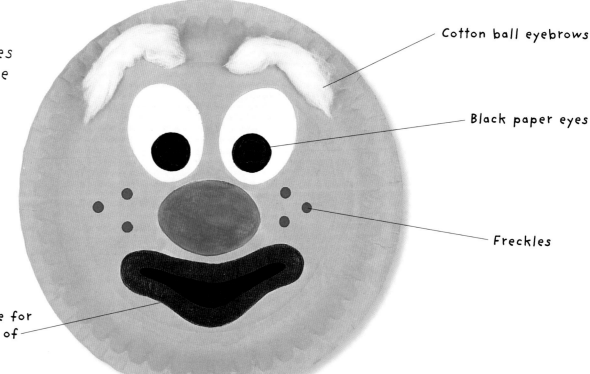

Cotton ball eyebrows

Black paper eyes

Freckles

Curved line for the center of the mouth

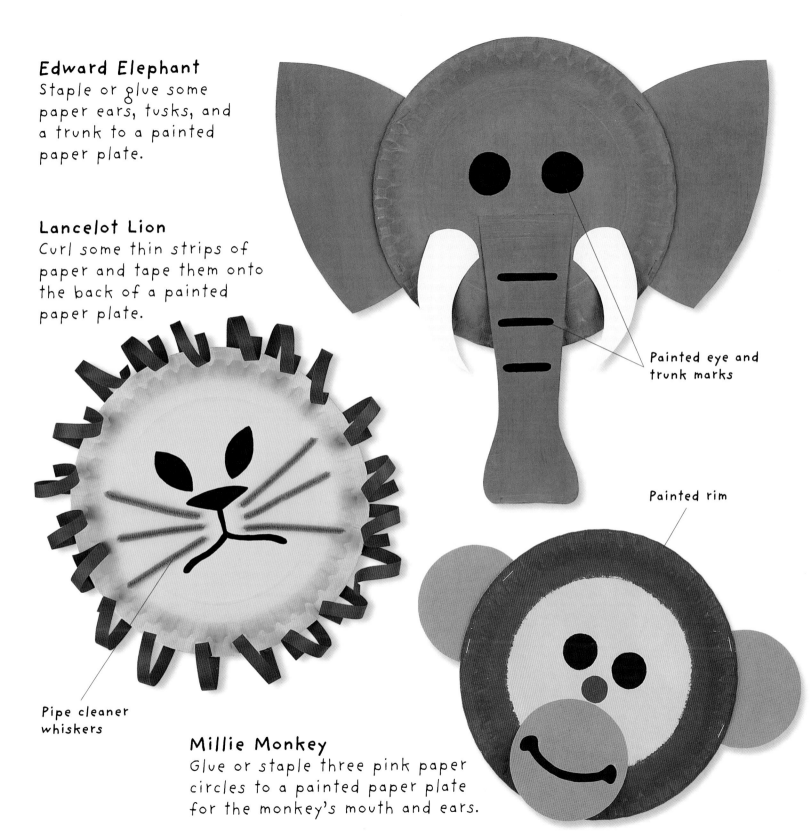

Edward Elephant
Staple or glue some paper ears, tusks, and a trunk to a painted paper plate.

Lancelot Lion
Curl some thin strips of paper and tape them onto the back of a painted paper plate.

Painted eye and trunk marks

Painted rim

Pipe cleaner whiskers

Millie Monkey
Glue or staple three pink paper circles to a painted paper plate for the monkey's mouth and ears.

Flags and Banners

You will need: construction paper, paints, scissors, and a paint brush or sponge.

1 Cut out a triangle from construction paper.

2 Then cut out lots of shapes from construction paper to use as stencils.

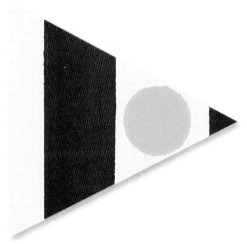

3 Paint or sponge through the stencils onto the triangle to make a flag.

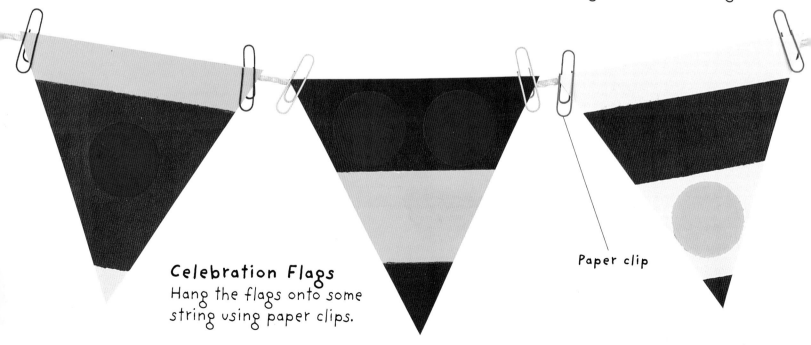

Celebration Flags
Hang the flags onto some string using paper clips.

Paper clip

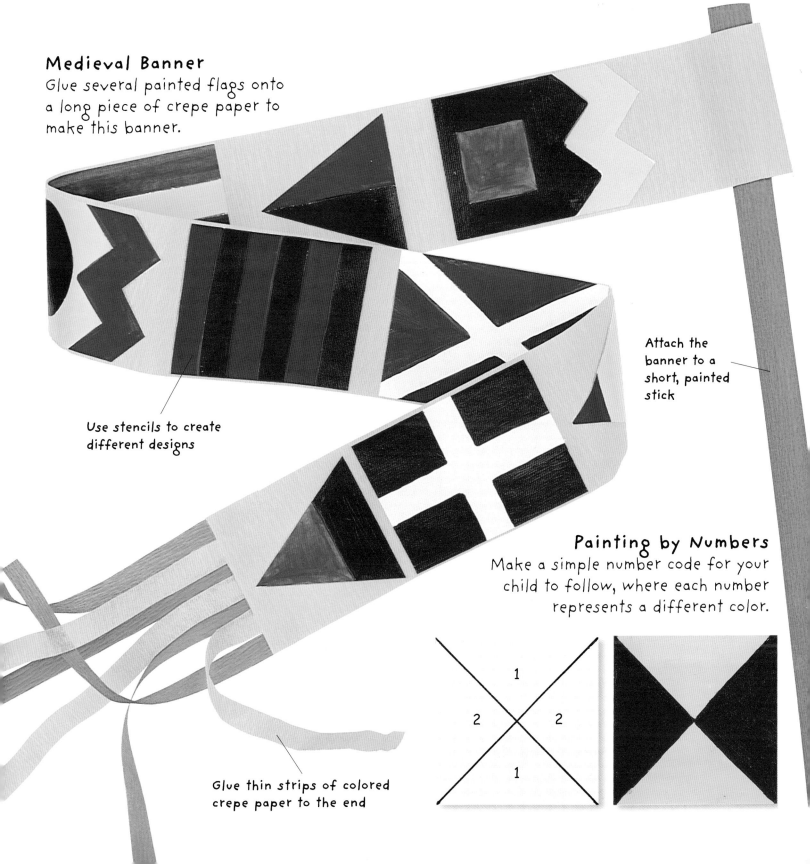

Medieval Banner
Glue several painted flags onto a long piece of crepe paper to make this banner.

Use stencils to create different designs

Attach the banner to a short, painted stick

Glue thin strips of colored crepe paper to the end

Painting by Numbers
Make a simple number code for your child to follow, where each number represents a different color.

1

2   2

1

Vegetable Prints

You will need: vegetables, knife, pencil, paper plates, paints, and a paint brush.

  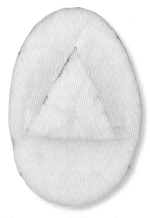

1 Put together a collection of vegetables such as the ones shown above

2 Cut a potato in half and draw a triangle onto the side that has been cut.

3 Cut around the drawn shape leaving the triangle raised in the center.

4 Dip the potato in paint. Press the potato onto a piece of paper. Try out other colors and shapes as well.

Potato Prints
Use basic potato prints to put together pictures like the boats and dinosaurs here.

Letter and Envelope

Dip a piece of celery and the sliced end of a leek into paint to create this decorative border.

Two celery prints made into a red 'kiss' shape

Gift Label

Use a broccoli floret cut in half to make this unusual label.

Christmas ribbon

Sprinkling of gold glitter

Wrapping Paper

Make your own stunning wrapping paper designs using vegetable prints and plain brown paper.

Triangular potato prints

Sponge effect using the end of some broccoli

Pasta Jewelry

You will need: pasta, paints, paint brush, glitter, glaze or varnish, and a pipe cleaner.

     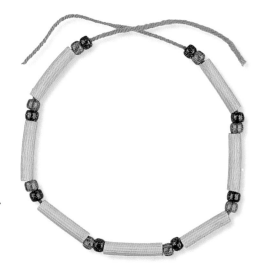

1 Paint pasta shapes you can thread, applying more than one coat if necesssary.

2 Brush the shapes with glaze if you have some and sprinkle glitter over them.

3 Thread the pasta onto a pipe cleaner or some string and tie the ends together.

Pasta and Bead Necklace
Try mixing pasta shapes with beads on some colored yarn.

Identity Necklace
Glue painted alphabet pasta onto poster board or foam. Punch a hole at each end. Thread some ribbon through.

Money Box

You will need: pasta, paint, paint brush, wrapping paper, scissors, glue, tape, and a box.

1 Paint half the shells gold and half of them silver.

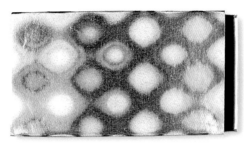

2 Cover the box with silver wrapping paper leaving the ends of the box free.

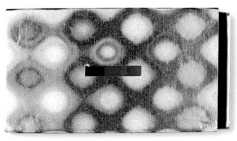

3 Make a hole in the lid of the box large enough to put coins through.

4 Glue the pasta shells onto the sides of the box and use it as a money box.

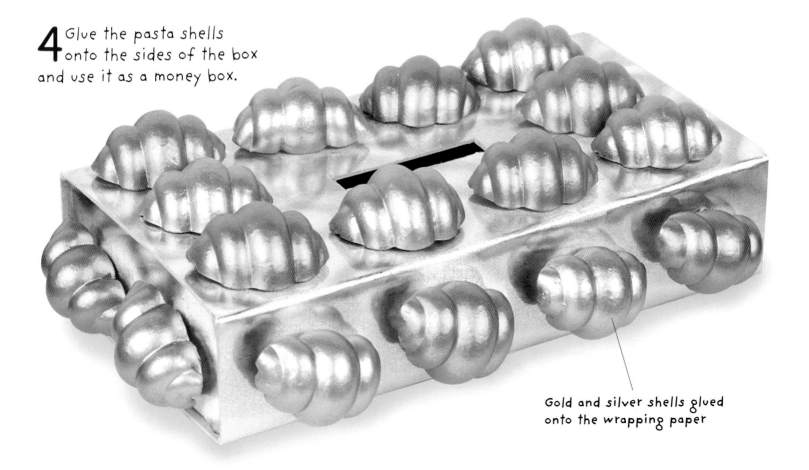

Gold and silver shells glued onto the wrapping paper

Caterpillar Pull-along

You will need: cardboard tubes, poster board, pipe cleaner, yarn, paint, paint brush, scissors, buttons, glue, hole punch, and beads.

1 Paint four cardboard tubes either using the same or different colors.

2 Cut out a poster board circle for the face and four curved shapes like the one shown.

3 Paint both sides of the shapes. Punch a hole in the center of each one.

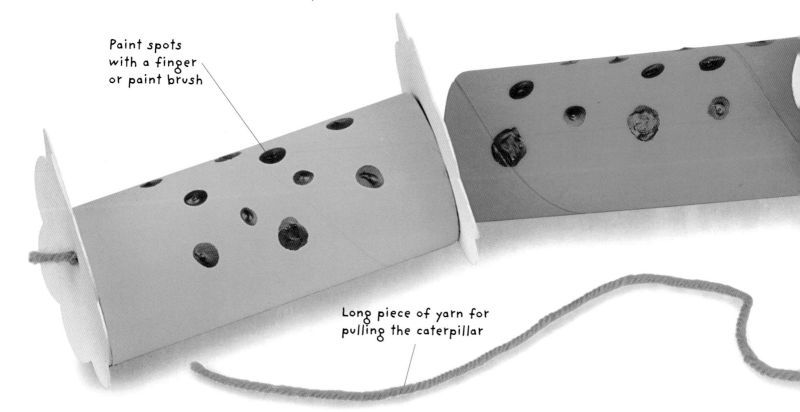

Paint spots with a finger or paint brush

Long piece of yarn for pulling the caterpillar

4 Glue on two buttons for the caterpillar's eyes and draw on a mouth.

5 Thread all the pieces onto a piece of yarn in the order shown. Add a bead for the nose and then tie a knot, leaving a long length of yarn for pulling the caterpillar along.

6 Tie a knot at the other end to hold the whole caterpillar shape together. Add any final decorative details such as spots and pipe cleaner feelers.

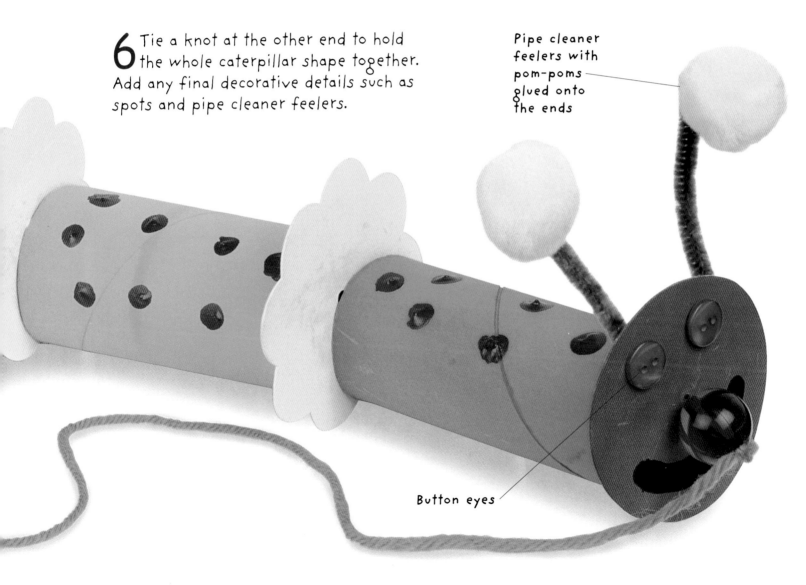

Pipe cleaner feelers with pom-poms glued onto the ends

Button eyes

Painting Gallery

Busy Bee by Maria

Pink Pig by Chuck

Hal's Footprints

Lisa's Pasta Necklace

paper

Paper Points

 The activities are designed for adults and children to do together. With a closet or a box full of craft supplies and a spare ten minutes, it's amazing what you can create!

 The activities should take about ten minutes once the materials have been assembled. Every child is different and often a project is worth continuing beyond the time limit.

 Step-by-step instructions are usually followed by examples showing how to extend the activities. If you don't have the exact materials, use anything suitable you have on hand.

 Warning: All steps involving scissors or sharp objects should be performed by adults, not children.

Paper Practice

Draw solid or dotted lines on any kind of paper for your child to cut along.

Let your child progress from cutting straight lines to diagonal, block, and wavy lines. Children should always use safety scissors.

Paper Closet

Keep a closet full of supplies for your paper activities.

Essentials

If you only have a few craft items at home, these are the ones to buy. Pads of paper in assorted colors, scissors, glue, water-soluble paint, crayons, and brushes are ideal.

Luxury Items

Glitter, feathers, stickers, and pipe cleaners are some of the many supplies that will add magic to your child's artwork!

Things to Collect

Recycle some of the materials around the home that can be used in artwork projects such as foil, bubble wrap, poster board, ribbon, and pieces of string.

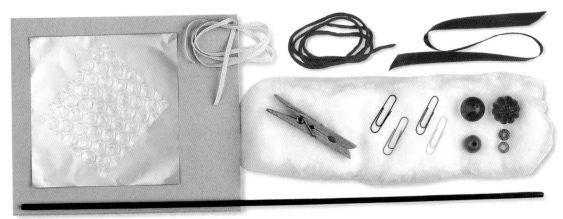

Paper Chains

You will need: construction paper, crayons, scissors, cotton balls, glue, and yarn.

1 Fold a small square piece of heavy paper backward and forward several times.

2 Draw the outline of a face on the front making sure that the ears reach the edge.

3 Cut out the face but not the sides of the ears. The ears join all the faces together.

4 Open up the paper to reveal the faces. Decorate each one with different details.

Cotton balls for white fluffy hair

Short strands of colored yarn for spiky hair

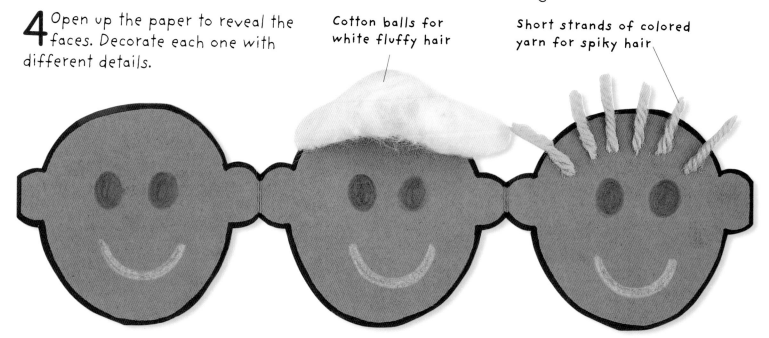

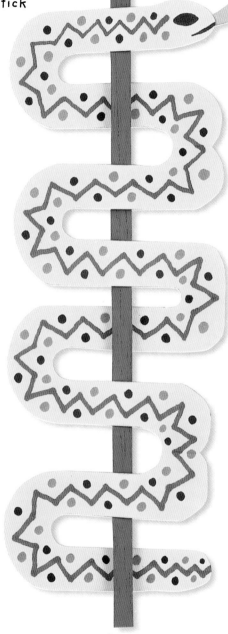

Wrap the snake around a painted stick

Make the perch act as the link between the birds

Bobby, Bert, and Bill
Fold some paper and cut the outline of a bird sitting on its perch. Open the chain, decorate the birds, and add tail feathers.

Lizzie, Lily, Laura, Lucy, and Loretta!
Paint the heads of the ladybugs black and make their spots out of small pieces of black tissue paper.

Sammy Snake
On folded paper, draw a loop shape for the snake's body. Cut it out, open up the paper, and then decorate the snake.

Paper Folding

You will need: paper, scissors, glue, tape, pipe cleaners, pom-poms, and beads.

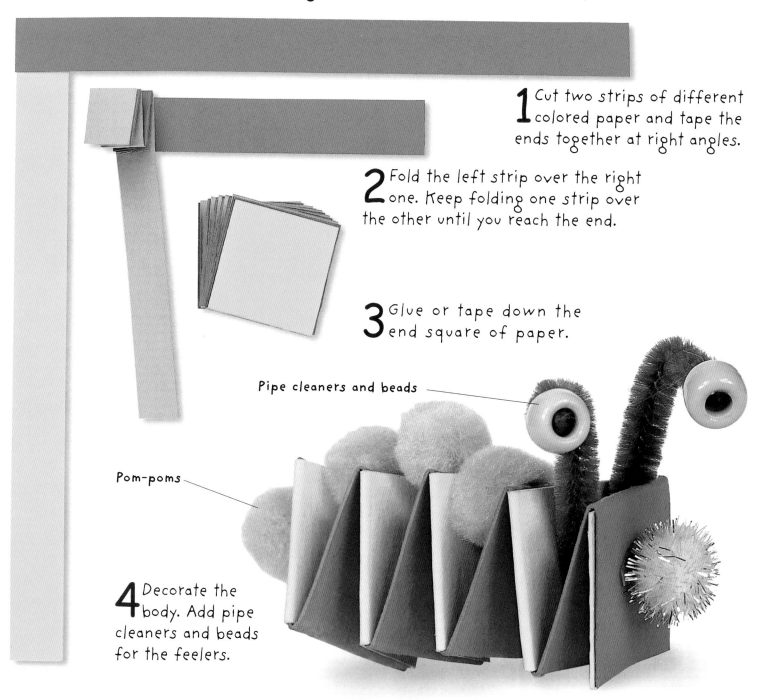

1 Cut two strips of different colored paper and tape the ends together at right angles.

2 Fold the left strip over the right one. Keep folding one strip over the other until you reach the end.

3 Glue or tape down the end square of paper.

Pipe cleaners and beads

Pom-poms

4 Decorate the body. Add pipe cleaners and beads for the feelers.

Crazy Bird!
Making this bird is much easier than it looks. It is three sections of folded paper stuck together plus some feathers.

Cut a square of yellow paper for the mouth

Pom-pom eyes

Use two wide pieces of paper for the body

Attach feathers for the wings

Make each leg from two thin strips of paper

Use orange and black paper to make the wasp's body

Winifred the Wasp
Use thin white paper folded backward and forward to make the wasp's wings.

Beads stuck on the end of pipe cleaners for the feelers

The Flower Garden

You will need: tissue paper, construction paper, scissors, glue, sticks, and pom-poms.

Bush

1 Draw and cut out a bush shape from green paper.

2 Roll up small pieces of tissue paper and glue them onto the bush.

Flowers

1 Cut out a simple flower shape from tissue paper. Then repeat this shape using two other colors of tissue paper.

2 Glue each shape to white paper. Then glue all the shapes together.

3 Attach the flower to a green stick and glue a pom-pom to the center.

Tree

1 Cut out a tree top from green paper and a trunk from brown paper. Glue the two shapes together.

2 Roll up small pieces of red tissue paper for apples and glue them to the tree.

My Back Yard
Glue the flowers, trees, and bushes on white paper to make a beautiful picture.

My Special Books

You will need: paper, hole punch, ribbon, felt, buttons, beads, glue, and a pipe cleaner.

1 Fold four sheets of white paper and a colored one in half. Punch two holes on one side.

2 Thread some ribbon through the holes and tie a bow. It is even faster to just staple down one side.

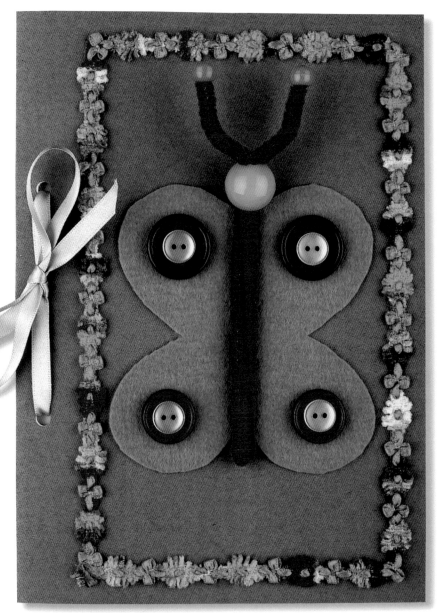

3 Decorate the front of the book with whatever materials you have available.

an antelope

a zebra

My First Photo Album
Use these books for first drawing books,
photo albums, storybooks, and ABC books.

Decorative stickers

Black paper can be very effective for displaying photos.

abc book

My First ABC Book
Draw a different picture for
each letter of the alphabet.

a

b

X-ray Images

You will need: paper, tissue paper, scissors, glue, white crayon, paint brush, and paint.

1 Glue a piece of black tissue paper onto some plain white paper or poster board.

2 Draw an outline of a hand and wrist with a white crayon.

3 Paint some hand bones using white paint. You could try doing a whole skeleton if you wanted to!

Sparkling Crown

You will need: poster board, foil, tape, scissors, glue, sequins, and pom-poms.

1 Measure the largest part of your child's head. Cut a band of poster board slightly longer than this measurement.

2 Cover one side of the poster board with foil taping the edges at the back.

3 Roll three strips of foil into silver strands or cover three straws with foil. Glue or tape them to the band.

4 Decorate the crown with sequins and pom-poms. Bend the crown to fit and tape it on the inside.

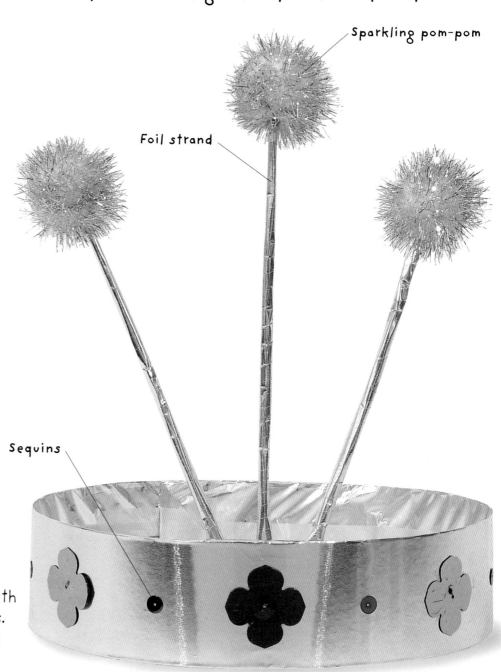

Sparkling pom-pom

Foil strand

Sequins

Mr. Moose

You will need: poster board or construction paper, scissors, glue, elastic, and a hole punch.

1 Cut a moose head out of brown poster board. Punch a small hole on each side.

2 Glue on the oval nostril and eye shapes. Cut out the eye holes.

3 Cut out two antlers from poster board. They can be simpler shapes to these.

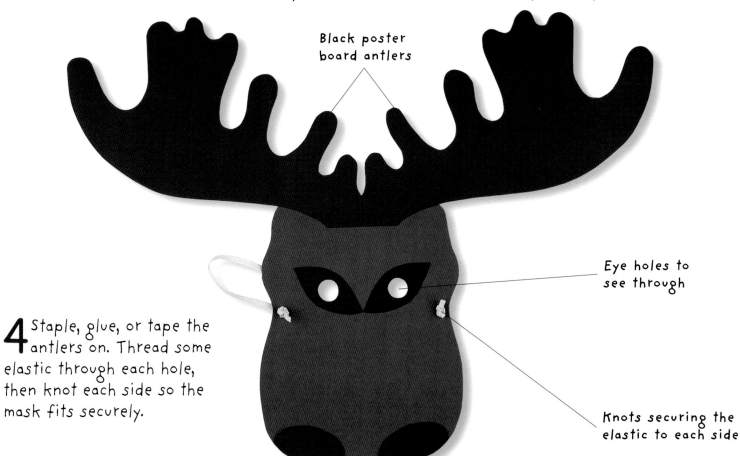

Black poster board antlers

Eye holes to see through

Knots securing the elastic to each side

4 Staple, glue, or tape the antlers on. Thread some elastic through each hole, then knot each side so the mask fits securely.

Mrs. Jumbo

You will need: colored poster board or paper, scissors, glue, and a short stick.

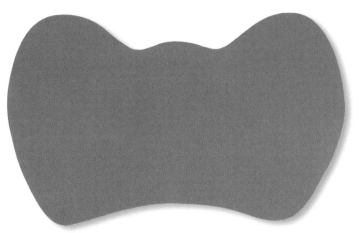

1 Cut out an elephant's head from a large piece of gray poster board or paper.

2 Next, cut out the elephant's ears, trunk, tusks, and eyes.

Cut out two eye holes

Attach the head to a stick so that the elephant's head can be used as a mask

3 Glue or staple all the shapes together like this.

Paper Airplane

You will need: paper, scissors, glue, and a paper clip.

1 Fold a piece of paper in half lengthwise with the fold lying at the bottom.

2 Next, fold down the two upper corners at one end to form a right angle.

3 Fold each side in half, press down, and then open the wings out slightly.

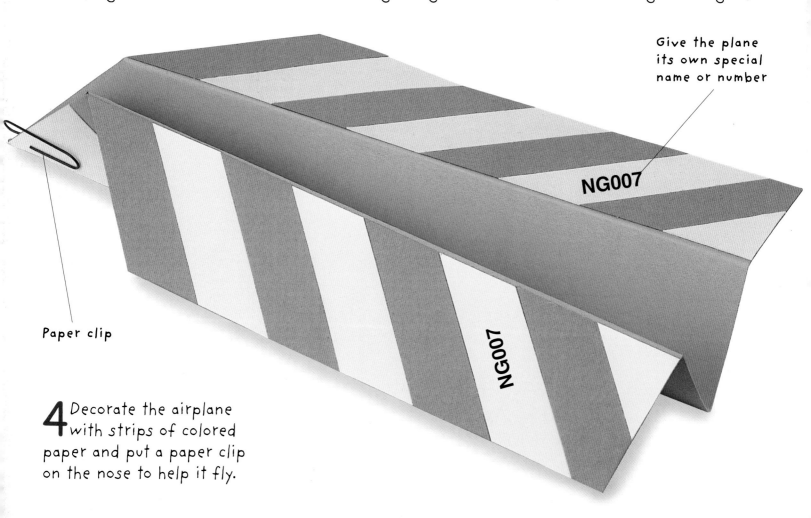

Give the plane its own special name or number

NG007

Paper clip

4 Decorate the airplane with strips of colored paper and put a paper clip on the nose to help it fly.

Space Adventure

You will need: poster board, paper, tissue paper, scissors, tape, and glue.

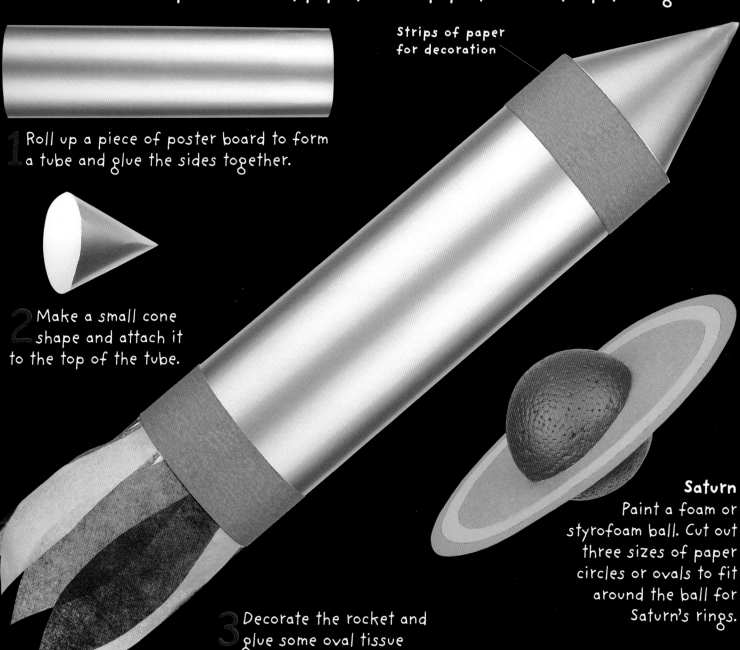

Strips of paper for decoration

1 Roll up a piece of poster board to form a tube and glue the sides together.

2 Make a small cone shape and attach it to the top of the tube.

3 Decorate the rocket and glue some oval tissue paper flames to the bottom.

Saturn
Paint a foam or styrofoam ball. Cut out three sizes of paper circles or ovals to fit around the ball for Saturn's rings.

Animal Clips

You will need: clothes pins, poster board or construction paper, glue, and a pom-pom.

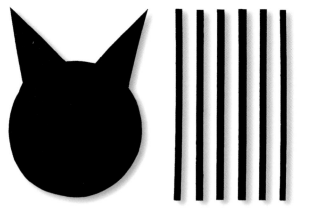

1 Cut out a cat's head and whiskers from poster board or paper.

2 Glue the whiskers onto the face. Draw in or cut out two eyes and a mouth from some paper.

Painted clothes pin

Cat's face glued to a clothes pin

3 Glue the cat's face onto a painted clothes pin. Finally, glue on the cat's nose.

Sparkling pom-pom nose

Freddie Frog
Make the frog's eyes from beads pushed onto the ends of a pipe cleaner.

Sid the Spider
Use the animal clips to hold party invitations or drawings.

Maisie Mouse
Pink felt works well for the ears of lots of different animals.

Party Invitation
You are invited to a party
On: February 24
At: Jo's House
From: 3:30 to 5:30 p.m.
....
Thank you for your invitation:
I can/cannot come.

Art Gallery
Use a string of animal clips for displaying a selection of pictures.

Rainbow Animals

You will need: poster board, tissue paper, paper, scissors, glue, and bubble wrap.

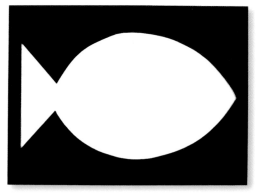

1 Cut out the outline of a fish using black poster board or construction paper.

2 Cut some strips of colored tissue paper to fit over the fish shape.

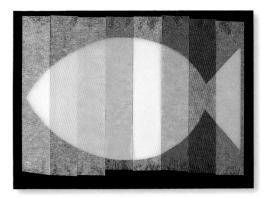

3 Glue or tape the strips of tissue paper over the fish shape as shown.

4 Turn the picture over and make an eye from black and white paper circles. Cut out seaweed shapes from green paper.

Air bubbles made from bits of bubble wrap

Crystal Caterpillar

Cut out a caterpillar shape and attach strips of tissue paper vertically across the body. Make a head out of a felt circle. Roll up small pieces of tissue paper for the legs and eyes.

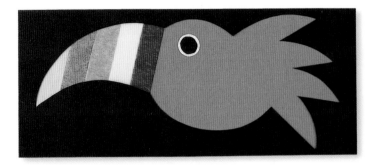

Cotton ball spout

Wally Whale

Cover a whale shape with blue tissue paper. Overlap sections to create a sea effect.

Tilly Toucan

Cut out a bird shape and glue strips of tissue paper across its beak. Use thicker paper to cover the rest of its body.

Dancing Figures

You will need: tracing paper, poster board, scissors, hole punch, and brass fasteners.

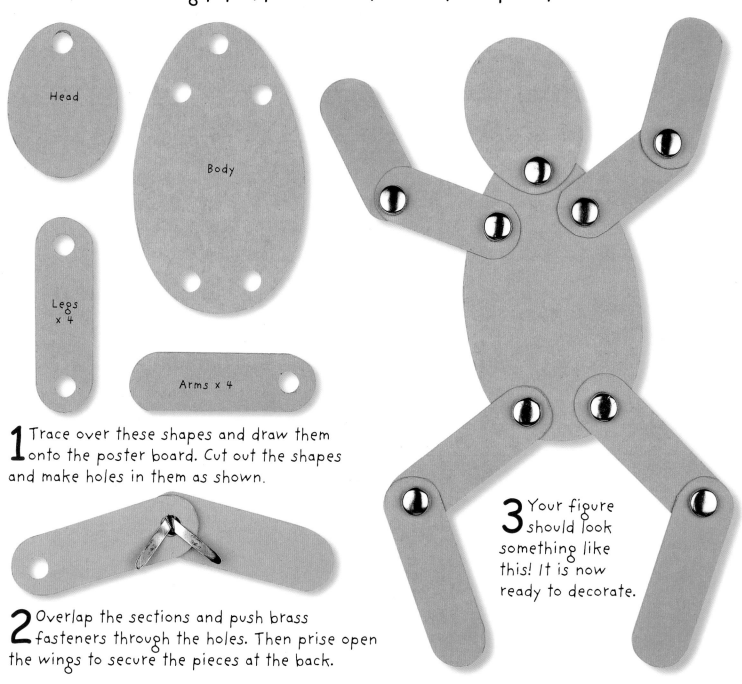

Head

Body

Legs x 4

Arms x 4

1 Trace over these shapes and draw them onto the poster board. Cut out the shapes and make holes in them as shown.

2 Overlap the sections and push brass fasteners through the holes. Then prise open the wings to secure the pieces at the back.

3 Your figure should look something like this! It is now ready to decorate.

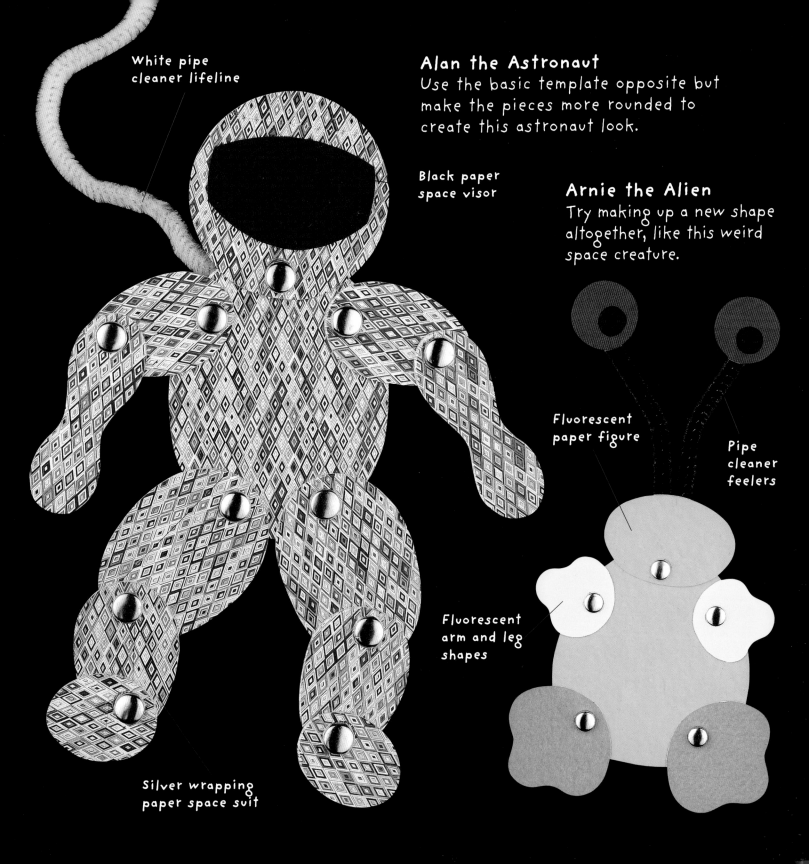

White pipe
cleaner lifeline

Alan the Astronaut
Use the basic template opposite but
make the pieces more rounded to
create this astronaut look.

Black paper
space visor

Arnie the Alien
Try making up a new shape
altogether, like this weird
space creature.

Fluorescent
paper figure

Pipe
cleaner
feelers

Fluorescent
arm and leg
shapes

Silver wrapping
paper space suit

Paper Gallery

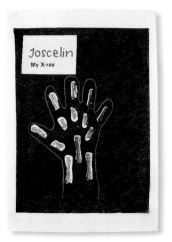

X-ray by Joscelin

Black Cat Clip by Dan

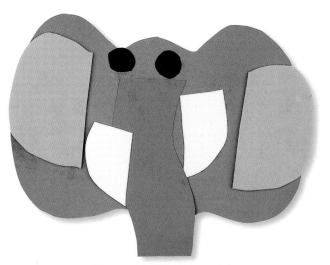

Dancing Doll by Mary-Ann

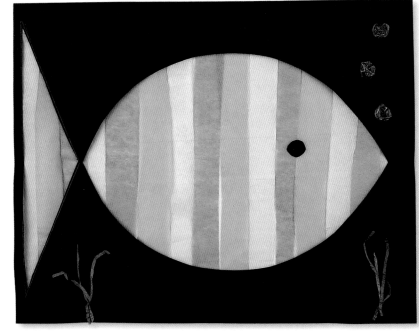

Rainbow Fish by Jack

Mrs. Jumbo by Lisa

craft

Before You Start...

 The activities are designed for adults and children to do together. With a closet or a box full of craft supplies and a spare ten minutes, it's amazing what you can create!

 The activities should take about ten minutes once the materials have been assembled. Every child is different and often a project is worth continuing beyond the time limit.

 Step-by-step instructions are usually followed by examples showing how to extend the activities. If you don't have the exact materials, use anything suitable you have on hand.

 Warning: All steps involving scissors or sharp objects should be performed by adults, not children.

Craft Practice

Before trying anything more ambitious, help young children practice threading and pasting.

Put some tape around the end of some yarn and thread pasta onto it.

Make patterns using beads threaded onto pipe cleaners or string.

Paste things like buttons, pom-poms, or fabric onto pieces of paper.

Craft Closet

Keep a closet full of supplies for your craft activities.

Essentials

If you only have a few craft materials at home, these are the ones to collect: paint brushes, paints, colored markers and pencils, scissors, glue, tape, paper, and poster board.

Luxury Items

Glitter, feathers, pipe cleaners, and special types of paper are some of the many supplies that will add magic to your child's craft work.

Things to Collect

Recycle everyday items such as cardboard tubes, egg cartons, buttons, and yarn for all your craft activities.

Sewing Shapes

You will need: paper plate, paint, paint brush, needle, yarn, and colored markers.

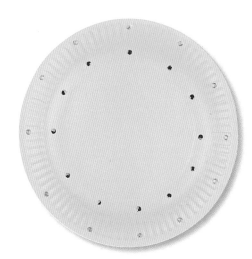

1 Make twelve holes around the edge of a painted paper plate and twelve more opposite on the inner rim.

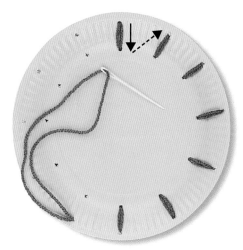

2 Thread a kid's needle through the holes and begin sewing as shown.

3 Sew in and out through the holes until the sun has all its rays. For older children, number the holes on the back of the plate, especially for more complex sewing patterns.

Give the sun a smiling face using colored markers

Bowling Pins

You will need: empty soda bottles, thick paint, paint brush, funnel, sand, and a ball.

Use several coats of paint if necessary

Add numbers and use them for scoring

1 Soak the labels off six plastic bottles. Fill each bottle with some sand using a funnel. Replace each bottle cap.

2 Paint the bottles using thick paint. When they are dry, line them up and try to knock them down with a ball.

Dinosaur Finger Puppets

You will need: felt, scissors, construction paper or craft foam, glue, and a button.

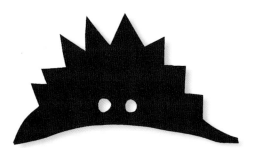

1 Cut out a dinosaur shape from paper or foam and make two finger holes.

2 Cut out enough small, square felt shapes to cover the dinosaur.

3 Glue the felt squares onto the dinosaur making sure that the base is covered.

4 Glue on a large button for the eye and add any other decorative details such as the ones shown on the opposite page.

Large button for the eye

Holes large enough for fingers to go through

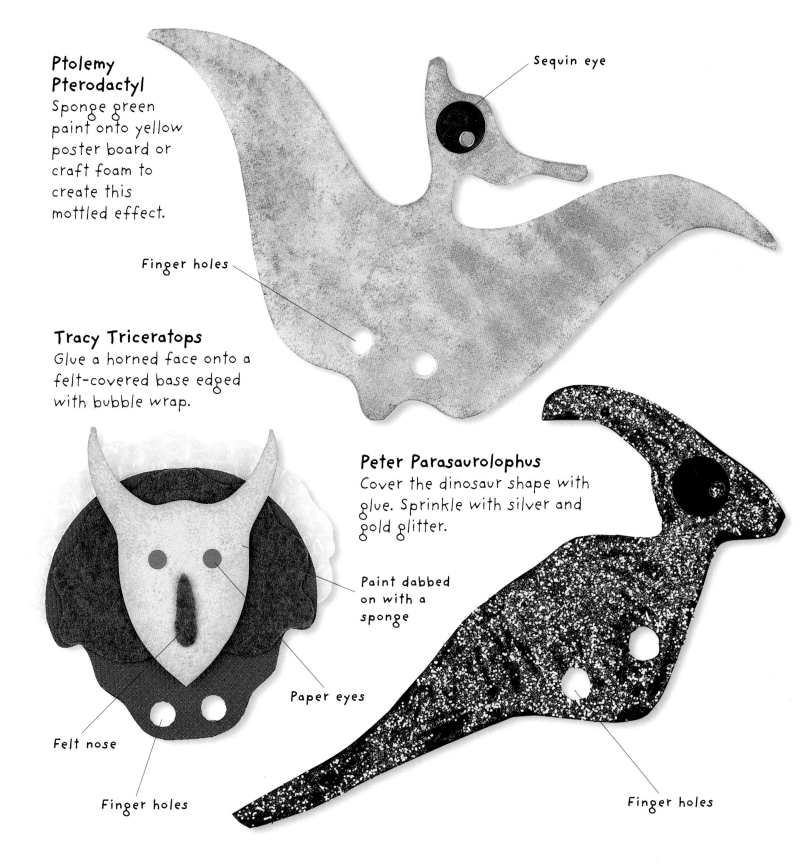

Ptolemy Pterodactyl
Sponge green paint onto yellow poster board or craft foam to create this mottled effect.

Sequin eye

Finger holes

Tracy Triceratops
Glue a horned face onto a felt-covered base edged with bubble wrap.

Peter Parasaurolophus
Cover the dinosaur shape with glue. Sprinkle with silver and gold glitter.

Paint dabbed on with a sponge

Paper eyes

Felt nose

Finger holes

Finger holes

Papier-mâché Plates

You will need: newspaper, plate, petroleum jelly, flour, water, paint, paint brush, and decorations.

1 Tear up some strips of old newspaper. Cover a plate with a thin layer of petroleum jelly.

2 Layer strips of paper over the plate. Brush on a layer of paste made from one cup of flour and two cups of water mixed together. Repeat until there are four layers.

3 When the paper has dried, trim the edges and remove the paper from the plate. Paint and decorate the papier-mâché plate.

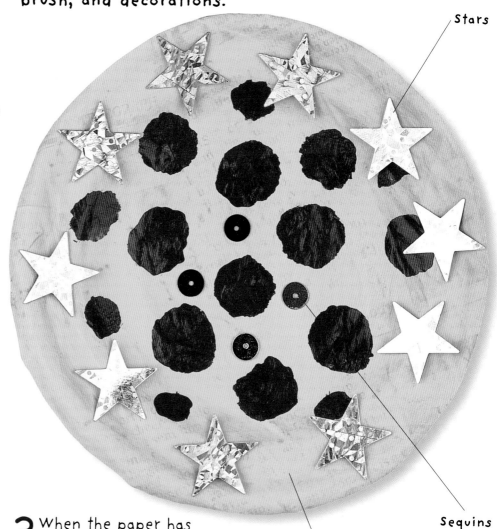

Stars

Sequins

Painted background

Face Plates
Use part of the untrimmed paper for hair and then paint on a face.

Fabric flower hair accessories!

Part of a bendy straw

Green painted cup and saucer with yellow spots

Play Cup
Make some papier-mâché using a cup with no handles. Add a layer of varnish or glaze if you have some.

Tea Party
Make your own tea set using different sized plates, cups, and saucers.

Bright colorful paints make striking designs

Fabulous Frames

You will need: poster board or paper, scissors, glue, fabric, tape, and a photograph.

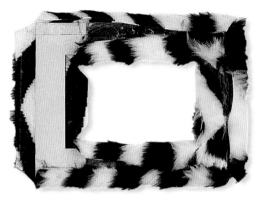

1 Cut out a photo frame from poster board. Be sure the inner dimension is slightly smaller than your photograph.

2 Glue the frame onto the back side of a piece of fabric that is just a little bit larger than the frame.

3 Cut out the fabric at the center. Make a small cut in each corner. Glue down the edges onto the back.

4 Tape the photograph to the back. Add a piece of string or ribbon to one side if you want to hang the frame.

Choose a fabric that suits your photograph

Jellybeans

Put jellybeans onto a poster board frame using double-sided transparent tape.

Silver foil

Love Hearts

See if you can match the shape of the frame to the candies or to the photo!

It helps to use candy you don't like in order to end up with enough for the frames!

Candy Collage

Big, bold candy pieces make an effective but simple design.

Thick border for larger candy

Spooky Spider's Web

You will need: paper, colored pencil, glue, straws, yarn, pom-pom, and pipe cleaner.

1 Draw a spider's web onto some black paper using a white colored pencil.

2 Cut straws to fit on top of the white lines. Glue them into position.

3 Glue two circles of yarn to the straws. Finally, make the spider by gluing eight short pipe cleaner legs onto a fluffy pom-pom body.

Place the spider over the yarn as though it is weaving its web

Fun with Flowers

You will need: baking cups, paints, paint brush, beads, straw, scissors, fabric, and construction paper or craft foam.

1 Find three different sizes of baking cup. Paint their sides and centers.

2 Cut out two oval leaves from paper or craft foam and punch a hole in one end.

3 Use a bead to secure the leaves onto a bendy straw as shown above.

4 Make a hole in the center of the baking cups. Push the cups onto the straw and decorate the flower face.

Glitter gel flower face

Use beads or fabric shapes for the center

Painted pasta eyes

Tie the flowers together with ribbon

Music Makers

You will need: shoe box, scissors, foil, glue, stickers, glitter, cardboard tube, paint, paint brush, hair elastics, rubber bands, and a straw.

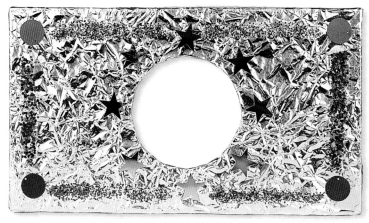

1 Cut a hole in the bottom of a shoe box, then cover the box with foil.

2 Decorate the box with glitter, stars, sequins, or stickers.

3 Paint a long cardboard tube. Put the hair elastics or rubber bands on as the guitar frets. Glue the tube to the box.

Plastic straw bridge

4 Glue a straw to the left-hand side of the hole, then stretch four rubber bands over the middle section of the box as shown.

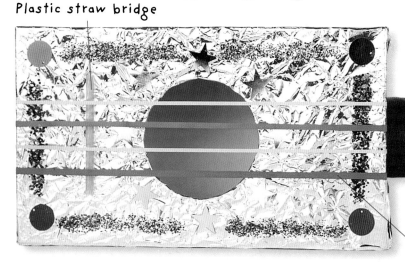

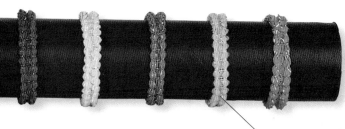

Rubber band strings

Hair elastic frets

Soda Bottle Shaker

Fill an empty soda bottle with hard, dried food such as lentils, pasta, or rice. Tape strips of paper that rustle to the end, then shake the bottle!

Rustling strips of foil and paper

Pasta, rice, barley, lentils, or popcorn

Band of card to cover the ends of the paper strips

Jelly Jar Xylophone

Fill some jars with different amounts of water and add some food coloring to each one. Test the sounds that the jars make by tapping each jar on its side.

Use a paintbrush or pencil to tap the jars

Sticky Pictures

You will need: paper, scissors, glue, foil, magazines, tissue paper, and marker pens.

1 Cut out a fish shape from construction paper.

2 Glue circles cut from foil and old magazines to both sides of the fish. Put the foil ones at the top and the others at the bottom.

Black eye, mouth, and gill

3 Draw in eyes, mouth, and gills. Glue strips of tissue paper to the tail. Suspend the fish from the ceiling.

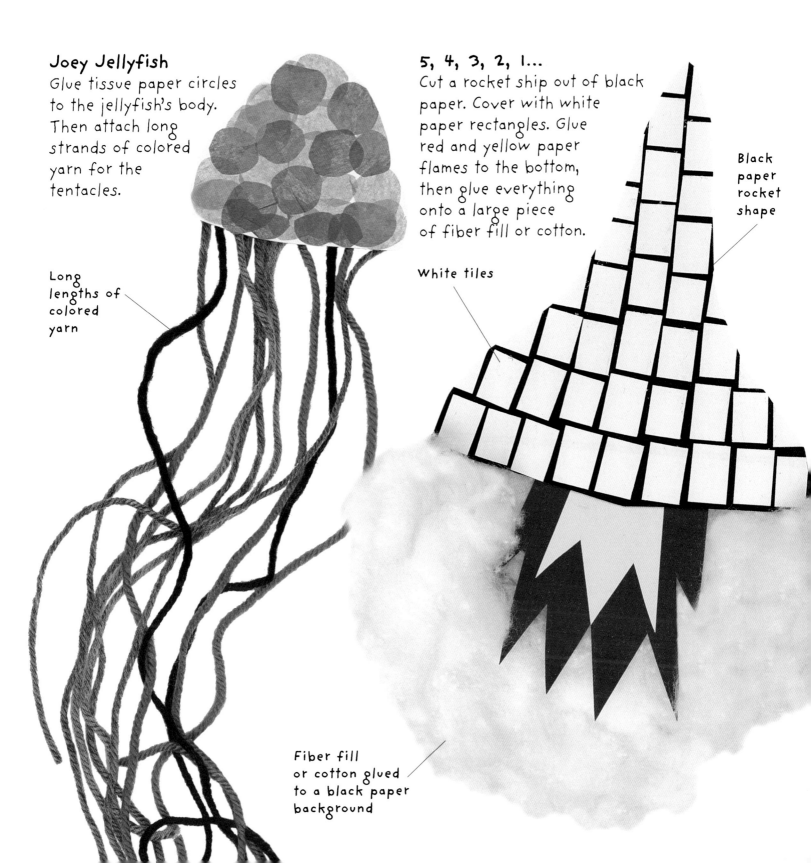

Joey Jellyfish

Glue tissue paper circles to the jellyfish's body. Then attach long strands of colored yarn for the tentacles.

Long lengths of colored yarn

5, 4, 3, 2, 1...

Cut a rocket ship out of black paper. Cover with white paper rectangles. Glue red and yellow paper flames to the bottom, then glue everything onto a large piece of fiber fill or cotton.

White tiles

Black paper rocket shape

Fiber fill or cotton glued to a black paper background

Picnic Train

You will need: small cereal box, matchbox, juice box, paper, scissors, glue, construction paper, foil, paint, paint brush, and a pipe cleaner.

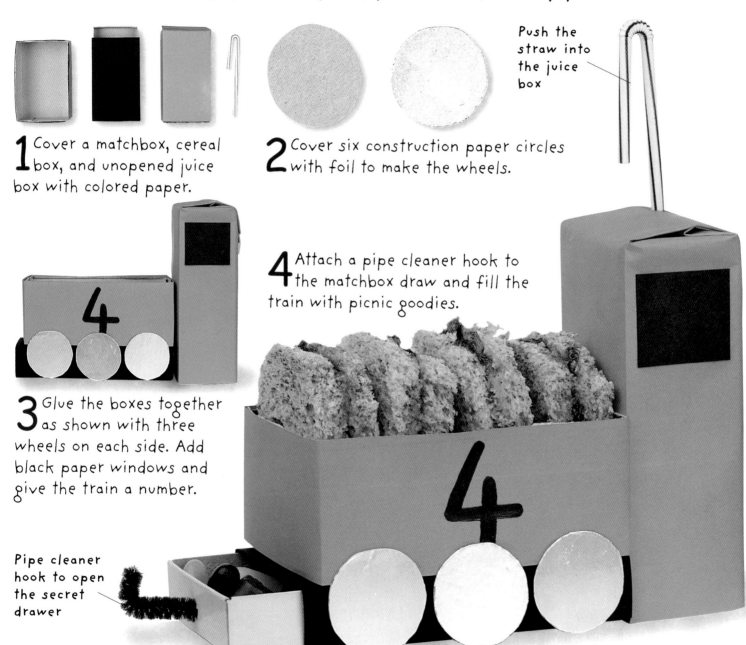

1 Cover a matchbox, cereal box, and unopened juice box with colored paper.

2 Cover six construction paper circles with foil to make the wheels.

Push the straw into the juice box

4 Attach a pipe cleaner hook to the matchbox draw and fill the train with picnic goodies.

3 Glue the boxes together as shown with three wheels on each side. Add black paper windows and give the train a number.

Pipe cleaner hook to open the secret drawer

Container Ship

You will need: cereal box, scissors, stapler, paper, cardboard tubes, paint, and glue.

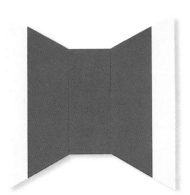

1 Cut out this shape using the bottom and two sides of a cereal box. Then cover it with blue and white paper.

2 Bring the two sides of the ship shape together and staple them at the top.

3 Paint one tube red, one yellow, and cover the last one with silver paper.

Colored markers

Paint brushes and scissors

Colored pencils

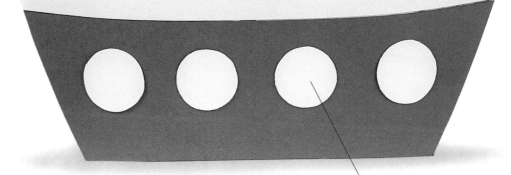

4 Slip the tubes inside the ship and glue on four paper port holes to each side. Use the tubes to store pens, pencils, and brushes.

White paper port holes

Bat Mask

You will need: egg carton, paint, paint brush, scissors, felt, stick, poster board, and glue.

1 Cut out the carton as shown and make two holes in the base.

2 Paint the outsides using orange and black paint.

3 Cut out the shape of a bat's head and wings from gray felt. Glue the felt onto some poster board cut to the same shape.

Gray felt bat shape glued to poster board

Silver stick for holding the bat mask

4 Push a silver painted stick through one side of the egg carton eyes. Then glue the eyes to the felt outline to complete the bat mask.

Crazy Caterpillar

You will need: long egg carton, paint, paint brush, pipe cleaners, scissors, paper, beads, cotton balls, sprout seeds, and water.

1 Cut an egg carton in half lengthwise. Trim the sides to make them even. Paint the carton orange.

2 Glue on pipe cleaner legs. Fill the egg spaces with cotton balls. Sprinkle seeds onto the cotton balls, water gently, and cover with paper until they sprout.

3 Make a face for the caterpillar and glue it to the body. The seeds should take about a week to grow. Keep the sprouts well watered.

Pipe cleaner feelers

Sprouts ready for cutting

Yellow paper caterpillar face

Pipe cleaner legs

Hats and Masks

You will need: poster board, tape, glue, glitter, stickers, tissue paper, stapler, felt, pom-pom, stick, scissors, foil, fabric, and feathers.

Princess Hat

1 Roll some poster board or construction paper into a cone. Tape the sides together.

2 Decorate the cone with glitter and make a border out of colored stickers.

3 Tape some tissue or crepe paper to the top and then glue on a sparkly pom-pom.

Yankee Doodle Hat

1 Make a tube shape using poster board. Cut the top of the tube at an angle.

2 Cut out a felt circle to fit around the base of the poster board hat.

3 Staple the felt to the tube. Push a feather in the hat and call it macaroni!

Love Heart Mask

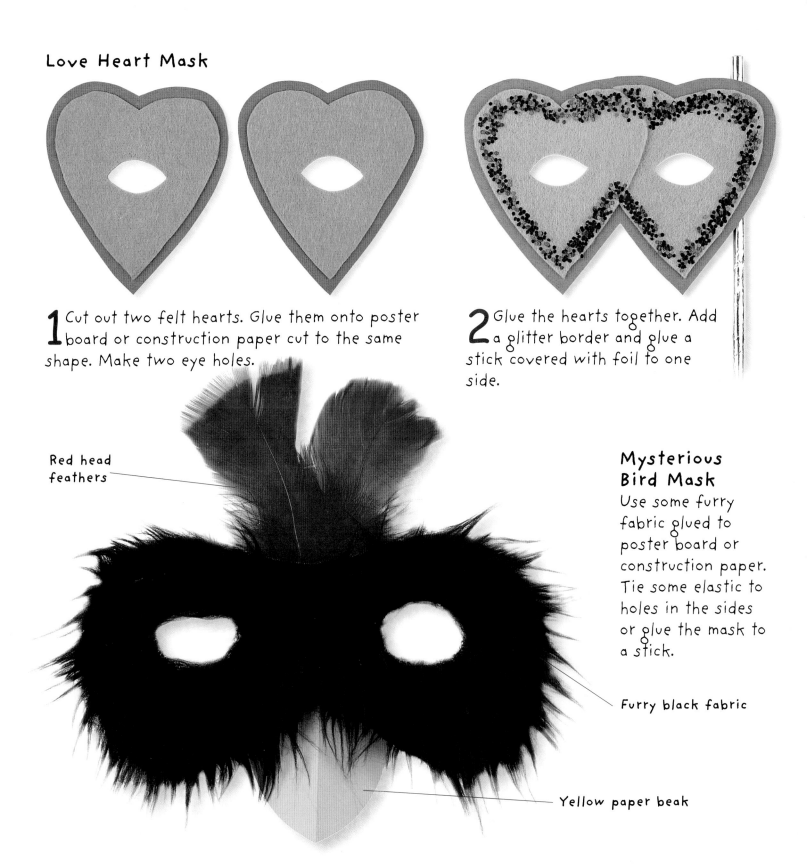

1 Cut out two felt hearts. Glue them onto poster board or construction paper cut to the same shape. Make two eye holes.

2 Glue the hearts together. Add a glitter border and glue a stick covered with foil to one side.

Red head feathers

Mysterious Bird Mask

Use some furry fabric glued to poster board or construction paper. Tie some elastic to holes in the sides or glue the mask to a stick.

Furry black fabric

Yellow paper beak

Craft Gallery

With thanks to all the children who helped us make this book.

Super
Rocket
by Harry

Fairy Plate by Kelly

Candy Frame by Conor

Flying Fish by Natasha